Poems4Nobodies

Ovidio Medina

BookLeaf Publishing

India | USA | UK

Presentation by *BookLeaf Publishing*

Web: www.bookleafpub.com

E-mail: info@bookleafpub.com

ISBN: 9789360943714

First edition 2024

*To my Children Dameon, Jaxson, Olivia,
Billie, and Max*

ACKNOWLEDGEMENT

First and most importantly All praises due to Allah. Thank you to my Mother and Father for always being honest and supporting me. Thank you to my Wife who walked through the fire with me and never gave up, even in the darkest times. Thank you to all my brothers dead or alive. This is for all the "NOBODIES"

PREFACE

This will be my first published work. Hopefully not my last. The thing about writing is I never feel complete because I have so much more to know and learn. So I just write and one day I'll have the material to fill the pages.

Beautiful Oblivion

I open with love.
That I use like a drug.
As an addict it's natural but stashed in it is
attachment issues I battle.
Fighting wars in my mind.
Trying to horde the things I adore, and indulge.
There's never enough I always want more.
Dopamine is validation,
And for your validation I'm a whore.

Gray Clouds and Black Sheep

They said I'm crazy.
They gave me medicine, it just sedates me.
If life is love and love is life,
Then why the fuck does she hate me.
Lately, Deaths the only thing that motivates me.
I'm so depressed.
Voices in my head,
Can't tell the doctor what he said,
Or I'll get locked up.
I know the ledge (knowledge)
So I'm drinking till I'm numb and go to bed.
Alienated myself so I'm alone again.
I'm trying to get back to my purpose.
Climb a tall building then jump,
Call it scratching the surface.
It's like I'm flowing on vinyl,
Writing in circles.
I'm the black sheep, out of place.
I don't get high no more,
My tolerance level is out of space.
This shit is deep.
All the coke on Tony's table,
My heart wouldn't skip a beat.
A thousand Xannies wouldn't comfort me.

If I say what's on my mind,
They'll come for me.

All I think about is death Lately.
I been manic, My therapist tryna separate me
from my family.
They're probably better off.
I quit drugs and they medicate me?
I'm playing a game you don't win, and I bet it
all.
I just don't care.
I'm trying to drink and say fuck it,
Everyone I know is dead or in jail.
I wonder why I'm still here?
Went from overdosing to strait sober.
Tell the other side my souls on the way over.
You have to stay awake to stay afloat.
When they say they love you they say the most.
So pay attention.
Myself is who I hate the most.
The mirror is my enemy.
Between sanity and sobriety, it's taking all my
energy.
I'm drained.
Looking for sunshine in the rain.

1986

Brainwashed minds, wearing stained washed
jeans.
You can't take that money to hell, the day you
leave.
When Allah takes your breath, it's the last day
you breath.
Keep trusting the same government that made
you fiends.
They pray on the weak, so I pray on my knees.
For strength.
And for all my enemies to awake, this hell on
earth.
Don't be the one these snakes tell on first.
Big brothers watching with satellites and the
meta verse.
Cell phones and megahertz.
You're all slaves to the game.
You better work, and not think.
I rather read.
All I know is broken homes and shattered
dreams.
I'm sinning.
Could meet death any minute.
So I'm thinking outside the box before I'm in it.

Bastardless Father

I've been alone,
 trying to master me.
Between fatherhood and relationships it's taking
a tole,
But there's no where else I'd rather be.
My oldest son blocked me,
Because his dad's a fiend.
I wish I could tell him nobodies perfect.
I had a dream.
Sometimes it works sometimes it don't.
You learn from rainy days to be a better person.
Look at me, talking like I know it all.
I'm still learning.
I have two daughters I'm trying to understand,
three sons I'm trying to reach,
And a good woman that I'm trying to keep.
My mind plays tricks on me.
I talk about life ain't shit,
Because she shits on me.
I tried to flip the script,
But it flipped on me.
I take the blame.
I tried to be sober and live,
But it ain't the same.

ode to Kurt

I'm on.
Psych meds,
And alcohol.
Heroin.
Ketamine,
And Adderall.

Sit and think.
Accountabili-TEA.
I'm a junkie.
I'm a fiend.
Sit and drink.
Accountabili-TEA.
I'm just bipolar.
Schizo.
Me.

Give me.
Kurt COBAINS.
Shotgun.
So I.
Can sigh.
Eternally.

I'm so tired

I can't sleep.
I'm a liar.
I'm a thief.
Sit and think.
Accountabili-TEA.
I'm a junkie
I'm a fiend

I'm on.
Lithium.
And Olazapine.
Weed.
Coffee.
Nicotine.

Scampi

You only get what you ask for.
You reap what you sow.
What you mad for.
You don't do shit.
But wish you had more.
Time never stops.
Forget the keys to success.
The doors never locked.
Just kick it in.
If all you do is talk
You're not listening.
People say I'm off.
Yes.
I'm off on some different things.
Too hot to be cool
Don't drink the Kool aid.
Mix your own.
Sharpen your tools.
To be smart enough, because dumb shit.
Always starts with a fool.
If you can't recognize who's who?
Its probably you.
Time to reflect.
We're all broken pieces.
In a world full of defects.

Unplug.
Psilocybin for the reset.
I been trying,
I been climbing.
I haven't peaked yet.
Suicide on my mind.
Self destruction is a reflex.
I'm still alive!
That's how we flex.

Digging my grave.
With a spoon I cook dope on.
So gone.
Too far to come back.
I had to let it go.
I couldn't hold on.
All praises to Allah.
It's cold out.
I seen my life flash before my eyes.
With no phone out.
I was just running.
With no route.

rUn

They only love what they can't have.
Want what they can't grab.
I'm feeling like I'm healing,
Then I pick the scab.
I don't want to die yet,
But I'm in the bag.
No brakes,
Just hit the gas.
The futures to bleak,
To live in the past.
They keep digging.
I'm drinking until I'm numb,
Now I'm hardly living.
Gun in my mouth,
Let the semi bust.
My girls mad,
Because she can't offer me shit,
I'm already fucked.
This is my life everyday,
They say I'm in a rut.
I couldn't tell.
I was sniffing perks,
Until I couldn't smell.
Open your eyes up,
Look at hell.

Heaven is just a mindstate.
The government passing laws,
To boost the crime rate.
I write for all my guys on probation who violate.
Snorting white powder,
They're pupils dilate.
You can hear it in my dialect,
I'm on a higher state.
Kids don't buy music no more,
They're trying to buy a vape.
All slaves to consumership.
Dhamer is a god now,
Its ludacris.
All I do is read books,
And ponder knowledge until it's crystal clear.
I want to shed my skin,
And disappear.
It's always "fuck it" let's ride,
What you are thinking scared.
You can't win if you don't play,
What do you think it's fair?
Mind, body, and soul I'm a visionare.
For the first time in my life,
I'm thinking clear.
Sober every other day.
We all have hell to pay,
Stop playing.
You need to watch what they're not saying.
There is static in the silence.

I'm an addict I haven't died yet.
It's just timing.
I'm sure it's coming.
I'm not around,
You better heard I'm bugging.
I'm a dharma bum,
Bigger they are,
Harder they fall
We all started at one.
If you hear this,
And you're scared?
RUN!

Nothingness

Question the world,
Like a child at bedtime.
With the same innocence,
Of not understanding the repercussions of your
actions.
So run!
And wherever it leads,
It leads.
Be receptive.
There is nothing more numb,
Than the thoughts of the collective.
Excitement lays in the danger.
The rush of slowly peaking over the edge.
The eye rattling vertigo.
Making your knees buckle.
Staring into space,
With clouds of ideas blowing through,
The atmospheric dome that is your mind.
With the occasional brain storms,
That manifest like a seedling to a sprout.
Into a plant,
Of theories outside the norm.
That feels freeing,
Almost euphoric.
To see the reactions of listeners,

When you question everything that they
precieve as concrete.
The only certainty is the end.
All the while knowledge was your friend.
That you used,
Consumed,
And spit out like it never mattered.
Walked away from,
And didn't look back.
Until you need him,
And meet again.
To play out the same cycle.
Always sitting on the edge of your
consciousness.
Dying to grow.
If only you'd take these blocks of thoughts,
And stack them on top.
To build a tower that leans.
Until if falls from ideas,
That crash into reality.
Particles glide in the air,
Like dust,
And rest in the ether.
To be broken down,
And replanted into the soil of questioning minds.
To bloom again,
And expand on what was.

Journeys

I see the lines like roads.
A page is a stage,
And anything goes.
From the heart,
To your mind.
It flows.
I see the lines like roads.

I see the ink like grass.
That needed seed to sprout.
Now it's deep enough to grasp.
I see the seed,
And how it grows.
I see the lines like roads.

When the world came to life.
They flow,
Like rivers and roads.
Or how the grass grows.
The cycle of life,
Pathways in your mind.
Live or die.
I see the lines like roads.

In the end,

They always say.
It isn't God,
You left astray.
It was love,
All along.
So if your alive,
Don't let it get away.

Fate-tality (Part one)

I'll blow my brains out.
Before I flame out.
This isn't art.
This is pain,
Transmitted through the pen,
This is how it came out.
I'm hardly holding on.
I'm hanging by a thread,
Or a noose.
It's getting hard to breath.
But I can't break loose.
I'm working until my back breaks.
Hardly making due.
Suicide on my mind.
I can't shake it.
I push the limits until I can't take it.
Smile in your face.
Internally I'm breaking.
This can't be fate?
Drinking till I fall,
Or sniffing "H".
Same shit,
Different day.
Everyday.
It's getting to heavy to hold.

I can't get away.
It's getting hard to live.
Im haunted by the things that I did.
If I ever got a bag,
Id give it all to my kids.
Before I go,
Let me crack this tall boy and smoke a cig.
The more I know,
I know,
I don't know shit.
Life's a blessing.
I'm about to blow this whole shit.
God can't save me.
The doctors medicate me,
Enough.
This is crazy.

Fate-tality (part two)

In the flesh and bones.
Made from the dust.
I seek thrills.
I came for the rush.
I'm a stain on society,
Sobriety is a cuss.
Right now,
Is as far as I can see.
A day in my mind,
Is like a week.
Trying to be strong,
Got me weak.
But I have kids to raise.
It's deep in these waters.
Life's a beach.
That Frank Ocean you better swim good.
Even when I've been down,
I've been good.
I can survive any weather.
Any terrain,
And it could rain.
It don't get any better.
I'm trying to maintain.
You probably feel the same pain.
Misunderstood,

Trying to overcome.
Russian roulette,
With a loaded gun.
No where to run.
Feed me the clip.
I'm just an idea,
I don't need to exist.
This is black tar,
You can shoot a needle of this.
Ain't nothing more evil than a bitch.
I mean mother earth.
I'm the son of her.
I'm from the dirt.
I don't give a fuck,
Like I'm cumming first.
You're too selfish.
But that's human nature,
You can't help it.
When Kurt Cobain's shotgun said "BOOM".
I felt it.
When my friend od'ed (overdosed)
All I thought was,
He had some shit,
And could've told me.
Addiction is a sick fuck.
I love my girl,
For loving me with this hiccup.
If my kids have to eat,
This is stick up.

Don't play.
Because if you aren't willing to die,
There's no way.

Pain. Won't. Stop

I don't know why?
This pain won't stop,
But it won't.
Shit got me by the throat.

I don't know why?
This pain won't stop,
But I'm broken,
And I'm trying to stay afloat.

I don't know why?
This pain won't stop,
But I'm open,
And I'm trying to save hope.

I don't know why?
This pain won't stop.

Alone

I been feeling all alone.
In a room full of people I know.
I know,
Times get hard.
I don't think I'm coming back,
This time,
Though.
Lost in the stars.
Waiting for the moon,
I'm trying to hide these scars.
I don't look too far ahead.
But I see death from afar.
It's like I been here before.
Or?
Maybe?
I never left.
I tried God.
I tried drugs.
I tried meds.
I'm not better yet.
Maybe?
It's all in my head.
I'm on the edge.
I'm feeling better off dead.
All I feel is pain.

It hurts when I smile.
Even when it's fake,
I feel restrained.
I'm sick and tired,
Of feeling drained.
I fucked up so bad,
You don't love me the same.

Dark Room

With the smooth hands of a surgeon.
On the page.
Create the wave.
I'm surfing.
I'm disturbed in the brain.
The meds my doctor gave me ain't working.
So I take acid,
And hug myself in a strait jacket.
Nobodies perfect.
Open my eyes,
Before the sun rise.
So I can pray.
I'm in too deep.
I think I lost my way.
So I reflect.
Sometimes the truth is hard to say.
But I have to keep it real.
Death is on my heels,
Even if not today.
I feel his breath on my skin.
Flesh of my flesh,
Blood of my kin.
Give me death for the win.
Since I'm losing,
The devil's checking me in.

I was born for the flames,
And absorbing the pain.
Using the name of your lord in vain.
Melting like candle wax.
My mind is chaos and random acts.
Of true evil.
Fuck haters.
I'll never lose sleep over "you" people.
I'll never change.
I tried to weather the storm,
But it forever rains.
They're turning urine into lemonade.
In a world where drug addiction,
And poverty is center stage.
So no lives matter.
I'm a renegade.
Just keep your mouth closed,
If you been afraid.
While you consume lies,
And fake news.
This is raw food,
For your consumption.
To properly function.
Destruction.

P.A.I.D. (Purposeful action invested daily)

I'm climbing trying to find the peak.
I reflect to define what's inside of me.
You have to watch alot of love,
Some is counterfeit.
You have to watch who you're surrounded with,
Because negativity can consume you,
If you're around the shit.
So I stay alone.
On my path to p.a.i.d.
Purposeful action invested daily.
I Meditate to relax the brain.
I used to get high to escape,
But there's no escaping the pain.
I embrace the flames,
And let it burn white.
While the pen scrapes the page on these blurred lines.
I write it for disturbed minds.
Trouble settles at the bottom of my half filled cup,
So I stirred mine.
Now it's too cloudy to see through.
Stop pretending trying to fit in,
Just be you.

People will make a move to move ahead,
Even if they know its wrong.
I been hanging by a thread,
But I'm holding on.
I want to see the end of this road I'm on.
The chosen one,
Strong like Hulk Hogan arms.
This shit will blow your brain out the back of
your head,
NO CAP!
I relapsed,
Then detached.
I'm back from the dead I can't hold back.
I talk like I seen it all,
But I live like I don't know.
You have to feed the seeds water and sun,
Or they won't grow.
So I take long walks,
And smoke weed.
I been going crazy,
These voices in my head won't leave.
So I conversate.
Breath deep,
And tell myself namaste.
I want to leave sometimes,
But I have to stay.

Time Papi

It's all just time.
Time being wasted.
Time being used.
Time being sold, and traded for.
But you can't sell time

It's all just time.
You can't go back.
It's an hour glass spilling it's guts.
Until the bottom fills up.
But you can't see time.

It's all just time.
Hands on the clock, ticking away.
It's symbolic to our hearts, because it sounds the same.
But you can't hear time.

It can't be sold or bought or traded for.
It can't be seen or touched.
You never heard it, but if you look close time is burning.

Slow drip

I'm waisting away.
Waisting away.
Trying to find my place.

This worlds so big.
That I get lost,
Or it just seems that way.

God counting down.
All my days.
I'm stuck in all my ways.
I'm trying to change,
But I'm stuck in place.
Trying to find my way.

I'm waisting away.
Trying to find my home.
I find myself Everytime I roam.
I think I lost my mind this time,
I think I lost my mind.

I'm waisting away,
Trying to find my peace.
Trying to grab what I love,
But it's out my reach.

You don't hear me when I speak,
But you get mad when I lose my shit.
I think we peaked.
I'm waisting away.

Obliviously beautiful

You don't find love,
Love finds you.
Everybody is concerned with the outside,
You have to work on your mind to.
I been trying to get sober for some years now.
Diagnosed bipolar,
The world still tears me down
Revert to old ways,
Then shed tears until I drown.
I'm lost again.
Lost in the wind.
I pray to God for my sins.
Tell the people I love "sorry",
For everything that I did.
I know the past is the past,
But I'm trapped,
So that's where I live.
It gets lonely in these long days.
Writing suicide notes,
While sad songs play.
That's the best thing I ever wrote.
I smile in the face of fear,
So you'll never know.
Making plans with my friends,
But I never show.

I feel better alone,
Or maybe it's just easy to hide.
Lying to myself,
Like this high is easing my mind,
But really it's just digging my grave.